Amidst The Wild Flowers

Poems on Love, Loss and Longing

NANDINI MURALI

Copyright © Nandini Murali 2022
All Rights Reserved.

ISBN 979-8-88684-582-2

Like the sliver of moon
In the third-quarter
Elusive, fleeting
On my cloudy
Indigo-night sky -
Your memory
Waxes and wanes.

Ever since you went away
The resplendent full moon
Is missing
In my indigo-blue night sky.

NOW AND FOREVER

Sunrise, sunset

horizon streaks

promise of dawn

This book is dedicated to my beloved husband, Dr. T.R. Murali, who gave life to many but lost his own, and my loving brother, C.R. Venkatesh (Venky), who loved life and lived as if every day was his last. Though departed, both live in my heart forever.

Contents

What They Say...

Nandini Murali's anthology of poems is a soaring elegy, a gentle lamentation, and an ode to lost love and eternal hope. This beautiful volume throbs with profound passion and naked yearning for what was and will ever be.

– Anuja Chandramouli, Author and New Age Indian classicist

Amidst The Wild Flowers contains reflective poems that are anchored in the interior landscape of the poet. Written in free verse, the elegant figurative language embellishes the book's gentle narrative. *Amidst The Wild Flowers* is an enchanting, poetic mosaic.

– Dr. R. Raguram, Senior Consultant Psychiatrist and former Professor of Psychiatry, NIMHANS, Bengaluru

This poetry collection is a potpourri of wild flowers where Dr. Nandini Murali has beautifully portrayed the breathing of her soul. It is a panoramic view of her inner self wandering through the garden of love and grief. The regional Tamil touch encases the poetic fragrance sweetly. *Amidst the Wild Flowers* in her own words will 'illuminate your being' and 'touch you in wordless silence.'

– Shalaka Kulkarni, Author, Marketer

How I Discovered the Valley of Wild Flowers

I still recall the wintry December of 2020. My earlier book *Left Behind: Surviving Suicide Loss* (Westland 2021) was ready to go to press. A deeply personal memoir of losing a loved one to suicide, *Left Behind* traces the narrative arc of how I healed and transformed through the tragedy to rediscover meaning and joy in my life. I had completed writing the book that had been gestating in me for two years and it had birthed itself in the public domain. I was filled with an overwhelming sense of emptiness and an aching longing that seemed strangely familiar.

A serendipitous conversation with Dr. R. Raguram, the well-known psychiatrist (who had also written a poignant foreword for *Left Behind*) was a turning point.

My landscape looks bleak—shards, smithereens and debris all around," I said.

"Look for the wild flowers… they bloom in nooks and crannies, in unexpected places," he remarked wisely.

It was a startling metaphor for renewal and transformation. From that day onwards, for every single day spread over 61 days, I wrote one poem a day in two notebooks. The physical act of moving my hands across the page was an experience that pulsated with raw energy and vitality. The collection of poems that you now hold in your hands revealed itself to me as I explored the sacred landscape of grief.

Deep gratitude to you, Dr. Raguram, for pointing the way.

Writing *Left Behind* was intense and deeply healing. Doing so helped me not only survive but also thrive and flourish. Throughout the writing of the book, my uncle, Dr. C.R. Kannan, was my writing coach, editor, therapist, best friend and uncle—all rolled in one.

Deep gratitude, Kannan Uncle, you permeate the book and my life with your subtle fragrance and gentle wisdom.

My parents, Sudha Raman and C.R. Raman—I am what I am today because of your value-based approach to life. Your indomitable courage, grace, dignity and wisdom continue to be my *Akshaya Patra*, the inexhaustible cornucopia of treasures from which I replenish myself, moment by moment.

My late mama P.S. Ranganathan, for constantly having reminded us to bow down to *Bhagavad Sankalpam*—the Divine Will—in letter and spirit.

Dr. T.R. Murali, I will continue to search for you amidst the wild flowers… your passion, precision and poise are my sources of amazement and wonder.

C.R. Venkatesh (Venky), a landslide has wiped away swathes of my childhood with your passing. You were a slice of sunshine flecked with the colours of the rainbow. The fragrance of your presence will always linger in my landscape…

Bhuvaneshwari Venkatesh, my sister-in-law, for enriching my life and constantly reminding me that the power of less is more.

C.V. Anirudh, my nephew, for helping me imbibe life lessons from a young millennial.

Dr. C. Ramasubramanian, Senior Consultant Psychiatrist, Madurai, for reminding me to forge deep bonds with my creative core. Your generosity and resilience inspire me.

Mamta Fomra, for the gift of sisterhood.

Malli and Minnal, for being my four-pawed writing companions.

Sri Guru Rohit Arya, my spiritual guru, for his wisdom and guidance.

Swami Sukhabodhandaji, for his pragmatic Vedantic insights in a contemporary context.

Radhika Sunderraj, for her perceptive editorial inputs.

Kavya N. Publishing Manager, Notion Press, for her patience, and perseverance to ensure that the book is what it is.

Last but most important, The Divine, for permeating my life even as I strive to be a channel for creative energy.

Foreword

Life, living and loveliness

These poems about love, loss and longing are beautiful. I am honoured to be asked to write the foreword. Recently, I quoted Nandini in a speech about the changing dynamics of women power from victim to survivor to thriver. There are several tools for surviving and thriving. As Nandini shows us in these pages, poetry and beauty are also among them.

The poet tells us how her love, loss and longing are expressed and felt by all the five senses and reflected by all the five elements. Our memory rests in the collective remembering of our myths, traditions and tales—so we see Andal and Bheeshma too in these lines. It is interesting how the same word, for example, *Ananta,* is repeated but evokes different sounds and thoughts each time.

The poet, Bharatiyar, says that when he places his finger in the fire, he feels the exquisite pleasure of touching Kannamma. Love and pain cannot be separated. These poems too are telling us that.

This collection is also about life, living and loveliness. Nandini's life and this collection stand testimony to her courage. I salute it.

– Justice Prabha Sridevan (Retd.)

Justice (Retd.) Prabha Sridevan served as a judge of the Madras High Court from 2000 to 2010. Post-retirement, she was appointed Chairperson of IPAB (Intellectual Property Appellate Tribunal) from 2011 to 2013. She is also a prolific writer, translator and intellectual, and writes regular columns for English and Tamil newspapers on a range of social, legal and political issues.

Cobwebs

You
Cobweb my mind.
I try to clear you away;
Your wispy memories
Cling on
Stubborn as clingwrap.

Embers

Embers
Of your memory,
I keep stoking them;
Only ash remains…
Sacred ash.

Scent

The scent on your shirt
Lingers,
Reluctant to leave -
Unlike you
Who vanished
Like a leopard.

Nothing Matters

Skydiving
Parasailing
Scuba diving
Rappelling
Mountain climbing
Without oxygen.
Adventure junkie?
Heights don't matter… Depths don't matter…
Since you went away
Nothing matters.

Vertigo of Grief

Hypertension or High BP?
Hyponatremia? Or low sodium?
Vertigo? Or dizziness?
I wish I knew…
*Stedman** seems inadequate.
Black or White,
I yearn for the million shades of grey
That you snatched away.
Is this vertigo of grief?
Or mere dizzy spells?
Google says…
Results don't match my search.
**Stedman: Medical dictionary*

Lingering

Billion likes
Standing ovations
Rave reviews

Except yours…

You talk in silence;
Your presence
In your absence.

Salad

Puree of your memories
Blended in a liquidizer.
But you -
You prefer
To be a salad,
Raw and pulsating…
Mocking at my assimilation.

Inhale... Exhale...

Inhale... You...
Breathe in... You...
Exhale... You...
Breathe out... You...
My every rise and fall...
Every fall and rise....
You... you... and only you...
Poetry in pauses.
Pain in *prana.*
Whip up winds of nostalgia
Sweeping across
Hills and valleys
Of my longing and desire...

Is this the fabled *viraha tapa*?
That pain of separation?
Or just prolonged grief disorder?
Does it really matter?

When will I stem this longing?
When my breath stops
And segues into thin air…
Even then
You'd linger …
Like an unspoken word
A wisp of regret
A half-remembered song.

Wild Flowers

My tears are sacred
Let Her flow…
Be a sacred witness
Touch Her…
Even your tentativeness
Is sacred.

Wipe, wallow…
Don't outsource Her
To a box of tissues
However discreetly placed
or pushed towards me.

I find them
Synthetic, superficial.
My sorrow is wild
Wipe Her away with wild flowers… if you can.

Like the wild flowers
Blot my tears
Sun dry them on the seashore.

Let the oceanic indigo-blue,
Turquoise green,
Infuse their essence.

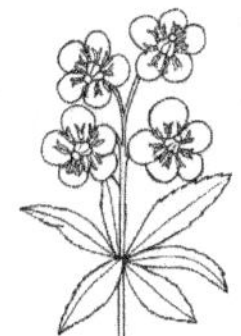

Sacred Tears

Let the oil spill…
Let the tears flow…
Sacred tears of joy…

Wayward… whimsical,
Will-o-the wisp.
Let them find their path
Towards You.
Fireflies in erratic flight.
Burning with passion,
Let me light your shrine
With the glow of fireflies,
Offering myself to you.
Nanda vilaku.
Illuminate my being.

Let my sacred tears of joy
Cascade over Your sacred body;
Your *tirumeni,*
Sacred, non-elemental.
This *tirumanjanam,*
A sacred anointment.

Leached

Leached

Of personal history,

A landslide

Eroded

Every redundancy in her.

Dislodged

Rocks and stones

From their niches.

Rolling down the abyss,

Splintering into a million fragments…

Vaporized thin air,

And then,

In the vast empty space within,

She bloomed

In the spaciousness -

Like the wild flowers.

Timelessness

He flung
Pebbles
Into her placid pool.
Ripples, eddies
radiating ever-widening circles…
Until
At one
Timeless moment
He
Coiled on himself;
Disappeared
Into folds
Of timelessness -
Ananta.

Solitaire

Webbed eyelids
Bat wings.
Solitaire ear-drops…
Her teardrops
Poised like the early morning dew.
A tendril of hair
Dares to stray -
Snakes down her cheeks
Inspiring
A solitary tear.
Solitaire.

Kurukshetra

I sprinted
Leaping off the ground
Suspended in mid-air
A gazelle on a mission.

A push, a shove,
Door yields.
I called your name -
A million *mantras*
A sacred *sutra*.

My cries echoed,
Ricocheted.
You were already my past,
Sprawled like Bheeshma
Arrows embedded
In the crook of your arm.

Left Behind
Alone
In Kurukshetra.
Trapped in a double bind.
Your Kurukshetra -
My *dharma kshetra.*

Intransitive Verb

My grief,
An intransitive verb
Foraging
In debris.
Groping
Compulsively
for you,
Amputated phantom limb.

Twisting and coiling
On myself -
A python
Swallowing,
Regurgitating
Rehashed memories.

Love at First Sight

Love at first sight…
The lotus and the sun
Blushed
A strange shyness;
Her breath was dawn.

Mute Your Paralinguistics

Mute your paralinguistics
Your um…mmm… oh… oh… ah… ah…
Stop your phony parroting,
Your empty paraphrasing.
I don't feel seen
Or understood.
Your words,
Opaque mirrors,
Silence your voice,
Quell your incessant chatter…
Stop searching for the right words -
Shining a laser
To spotlight my feelings.

Turn off your camera,
Dismount your lens,
Throw away your filters…
I do not need
Your picture-perfect images.
Nor your word perfect,
Letter perfect prose.

Only in your alexia
Can you hear me.
Ground yourself in stillness
Hear me in wordless silence.

Witness Me

Let our *swaras*,
Our breaths
Coil
Like *Kundalini;*
Arise
Ascend
In sibilant whispers.
Challenge me.
Like the *Lingodhbhava*
Let me touch the Source.
But, be there for me
Rooted in your knowing.
Let our *pranas*
Bounce off each other,
Intermingle.
Witness me.
Honour me.

Blackhole

Trapped
In the blackhole of grief.
Lost forever.
Like you.

Tangy Tears

My keyboard froze
Splattered with my tears.
Tangy tears.
Even your memories
Taste bitter,
Corroded.
Erase
QWERTY
ASDEF
ZXCV.
Robbed of my alphabet,
My fingers grope
Stubborn gecko
Lizard sounds
To tell
Your story…
Our story…
My story.

Stain Remover

You bled into my life;
Your memory
Stains.
I don't want to
Remove them;
Bleach them
Using stain remover.

Tattoo Artist

You wrote no poetry,
But engraved poetry
On your body
Like a tattoo artist.

Ménage à Trois

Ménage à trois
BPAD*
You
Me

Since you went away
Both BPAD and me
Are lamenting
Our lost partner.
Bipolar Affective Disorder

Mahabali's Anthem

You lit my landscape
A fiery flower pot
Bridging the earth and sky…
Incandescence.
I gaze
Vamana-like
At your
Cosmic splendour.
I grope
For fragments;
String the embers
Yearn to ignite
Your warmth
In my veins,
Mahabali's anthem.

Caramelized Grief

Butterscotch ice cream,
Bitter aftertaste,
Caramelized grief…

Missing the garden birds…
Raucous tree pies,
Chatty babblers,
Hovering near the birdbath
Overflowing with my tears.

Muted birdsong,
This silence of grief,
This *mahapralaya* of my sorrow.

Gossamer Memories

I try to entrap you
In my gossamer web of words.
You elude…
This grammar of grief.
You lurk…
In sentence fragments
Ellipsis
Comma splice
Run-on sentences
Whirls… whorls.
Poetry in pauses.
Loss in letters.
Pain in punctuation.
Wild flowers everywhere
Yet nowhere.

Solitary Tear

Before the next teardrop,
Before the solitary tear
Risks the flow
And streaks my face,
Let me fling
My foggy contact lenses,
My scratched spectacles,
My fragile filters.
Let my solitary tear
Cleave
Filigreed tributaries.
A delta of sorrow
Meandering,
Gathering wild flowers,
Oceanic offering.

Doodles on the Seashore

Doodles on the seashore
Tracing wayward patterns
Shapes, forms…
Karmic patterns
Dissolve in the waves
Leaving no imprints.

This elemental dance
Of surf and sand -
One and Two
Two and One.
No control, no force,
Just an invitation…
Such supreme yielding,
A graceful flow
Melting every trace of resistance,
An endless dance of joy.
Creation blushed
A crimson dawn.

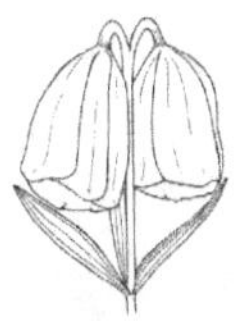

Scalloped Seashores

I dance along
Scalloped seashores;
My footprints
Etch the glistening shore
Erased by persistent waves,
Yet I walk,
Undeterred -
My feet crunching the cowrie shells
Along the contoured shorelines
Like the resilient hermit crab.
This *adipradakshina;*
My step-by-step pilgrimage
In search of you.

Flight of the Shorebird

The wayward wind
Tousles my hair
Kisses me
Billows my skirts
Lifts me
And drops me in unknown places;
Sacred spots…
A shore bird seeking its flight path.

Oceanic Breeze

Millions of sand grains
Lodge between
My tiny crevices -
The folds of my skin, on my feet,
The funnels of my ears.

The ocean breeze
Prises my mouth,
Folds my insides,
Fills me with strange, muted longings;
Embeds itself in my wet spaces.
Here, wild flowers bloom.
The oceanic breeze
Sweeps through me,
Atomizes my calcified memories.
I am swept clean.
The wind, my Beloved.

Sacred Geometry

You contour me

Lines…

Curves…

Ellipses…

Sacred geometry.

A *mandala* of possibilities

Pulsating

The still, silent centre.

Enter the Circle

Enter the circle
Cross the *dwara*
Subliminal
Sacred threshold.
Wayward wanderer,
Come, roam with me!
Sibilant whispers,
The music of the ocean,
Song of the stars,
Dance of the wild flowers,
Nishabdam.
Space. Silence. Spaciousness.

The Broken Door

You linger
On my threshold,
A stubborn scent
Tentative shadow
Flitting, floating
Phantom in the dark.
Tempting me
To play
Hide and seek
On your terms;
The tiger and the deer.

I crane my neck,
Fumble at the door.
You crouch,
Inch forward,
A swift silent swoop

Ambushing me.
My skin
Tumbles outside.
Crumpled rag doll.

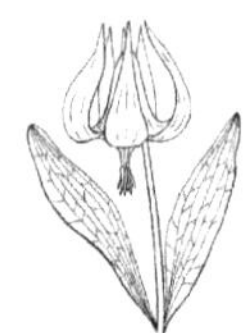

Postcoital Slumber

You transgressed;
Mocking,
Breaching barriers and boundaries
Until you can pump no more.
And I?
I clean up,
Sanitize, deodorize
Stubborn stains -
And still fumble
To fix the door.

While you -
You drift off
In postcoital slumber.

Left Behind

After you left -
Left me behind,
I am a writer
Wandering for words,
Yearning for the SVO* pattern
You abducted from me.
Transgressing like Ravana
When you,
I presumed, was my Rama.
"It's mine…"
I hear
Your entitlement.
I struggle to write.
Yet, SVO patterns
Linger
Like *vasana-samskara.*

My aphasic struggle
To cling on to SVO patterns -
A butterfly
Thrashing against the bell jar

Desperate for the tailwind
To lift me.
Let me create a new language -
Robust SVO patterns
Stress-resistant…

Hear my empowered voice
Peal like temple bells -
Your entitlement
My enlightenment.
Subject Verb Object

Sanguine Longing

My clothes flutter
Soar
Sail skywards…
Perpendicular rise
No pegs to hem
Nothing to stem the flow.

I bleed;
Inviting you
To wallow
In my bloodiness…
You sidestep -
Artful
Mountain goat.

Dry vagina

Drooping breasts

Nipples shrivelled like prunes.

Cracked river bed

Parched interiors

Wetness

A sanguine longing.

Be My Carl Zeiss

Time for the exchange.
Let me exchange
The magnifying glass
For the Carl Zeiss binoculars.

Let me dismount the lens
Throw away the super-telephoto lens,
Dismantle the camera
Throw away the tripod.

Instead,
Let me implant
The Carl Zeiss optics
In my eyes.
Carl Zeiss, your favourite optics.
Through which you gazed -
Passion, precision, purpose
Your tripod.
As you explored
The valleys and craters
Of people's pain and sorrows…

As you transmuted them into joy.

Couldn't you have turned that gaze inwards?

Never mind.

Come, be my Carl Zeiss.

Help me see.

Be my vision 20/20.

As my voice

Echoes across the realms

I'll show you

The panorama you missed.

Escape Velocity

Lift me off the ground.
Be my escape velocity.
Help me find
That moment of stillness.
Let me align with you
To lift off
The gravitational pull of grief.

Soaring on
The wings of my wisdom,
Tethered to you.
Soaring higher than the bar-headed geese -
Freedom from gravity.

Let the Oil Spill

Let the oil spill
Let the tears flow,
Sacred tears of joy.
Wayward, whimsical,
Will-o-the-wisp…
Let them find their way
Towards You.

Silhouettes

You recede
Farther and farther -
The ocean in low tide.
A reluctant
Wave on the sand -
Tantalizing distant horizon.

All I have
Are
Silhouettes of your memory -
Like the setting sun
Streaking the sky
In golden hues
Now golden, now gone
Forever.

Fireflies

Let the fireflies
Trace an erratic path
Towards You.
Burning with *Bhakti*
Let me light Your shrine
With the glow of the fireflies.

I offer myself to You
Like a *Nandvilakku.*
Illuminate my being.

Let my sacred tears of joy
Cascade over your *Tirumeni,*
Your sacred non-elementality.

This *Tirumanjanam*
A joyous offering.

Flight of the Flamingos

Can my adoration
Of You
Rise upwards
Lift off?
The pull of gravity
Air-borne…
Stunning synchrony
Silhouettes of wingspans
Showering sacred petals
Wild flowers
On Your *Vimana* –
This flight of the flamingos.

Unheard Melody

He worshipped
Her.
She bloomed
Sacred wildflower.

Their love
Anahata nadam
Unstruck, unheard melody.

Music of the spheres
For their ears only.

Vasishta and Arundhati

Moonlight streaming
across the ocean,
Shimmering.

Stars sprinkled
Like crushed diamonds
Across the indigo-blue sky
Sparking… twinkling…
Like our love -
Vasishta and Arundhati.

Framed Photograph

He was all
Constants
Straight lines
Right angles
Co-ordinates
Black or White
Linear arithmetic
1+ 1 = 2!

She introduced him to variables
curves
Flow...eddies... whirls... whorls... swirls...
Rainbows
Pauses.. silences...
The music of the rain
The magic of mathematics
1+1 = infinity or beyond!
Now that he's gone
She searched
For his beloved constants
And, instead,

Discovered the wild flowers,
While he
Flashes his amused
animated smile,
Hemmed in
A framed photograph.

Infinity

He flung
Pebbles
Into her placid pool.
Ripples, eddies,
Radiating outwards towards infinity.
Until at one
Timeless moment,
He
Coiled on himself
Disappeared
Into folds of timelessness
Ananta.
Her *Ananda*.

Seashells on the Seashore

She drifted
A wave in search of the ocean
A seashell in search of its song
A seabird seeking its path…

She embraced solitude -
A seagull
On its flightless path
Across the oceanic expanse,
A collector of seashells on the seashore.
She never found seashells.
The seashells found her.
Always.

Emergence

Wild flowers
Sailed, floated, drifted
Like the migration magic
Of rosy starlings
Exulting
In freedom
From the tyranny of time.

Her tears,
Metallic in mass and intensity,
Welled and surfaced,
Then, forgotten.
Subterranean Saraswati -
Surfacing,
Emerging,
Staking her claim
To discover herself -
Her ocean.

Andal's Offering

I clasp the Valampuri conch shell -
Right spiralling
Panchajanya
Reclaimed from oceanic depths
Like me.
Ground me in Your presence.

Primordial sounds
Swell from deep within.
This resonant music of the spheres
Rise and fall
Fall and rise -
This dance of surf and sand.

You whisper, sing
Secrets in soft sibilant sighs -
This Song Divine,
Your *Bhagavad Gita.*

I listen.

Your oceanic wisdom
Roars through my cavernous spaces.

The whole in a fragment
The fragment in a whole;
The wave in the ocean
The ocean in the wave....
I have reached your *dwara*
Enable me to cross
The sacred threshold.
Let me offer a garland of wild flowers -
Andal's sacred offering.

Anthem to Nostalgia

Mounds of coloured
Hand-shaped rice balls
Randomly placed
On crackling turmeric leaves
Resting on Amma's
East-facing
Padikolam.

The sun has traced
His trajectory
From South to North;
Sacred *Uttarayana* –
When Bheeshma chose
To exit his physical body.
Can I too
Awaken the Bheeshma within?
Abdicate nostalgia,
Even joyful nostalgia…

Start afresh -
Imprint-free
Glistening
A rain-washed
Banana leaf.

One for Sorrow, Two for Joy

The curtains flail,
Demonic breeze…
A deathly chill invades the room.
Huddled in the corner
Of a window sill
A large-billed crow
Fluffs its wet feathers,
Burrows inside itself.

One for sorrow… two for joy…
Fragments of a childhood song;
Fragments of my life with you…
Is there another?
No… you… you… and only you…
Just one… one for sorrow…
I cross my middle and forefingers,
Palpable anticipation,
A talisman for sorrow.
One for sorrow…

Rain descends
Rumbling, tumbling,
Chilling my bare-bones,
Drenching my memories.
Stray spumes caress my face.
I smile… memories
Playing hide and seek…
This dance; this *lila*
Of tears and spray.
Rivulets of sorrow
Thrash the ground,
Dislodge mud from the earth.
This *manvasanai*
The scent of rain on earth,
A lingering… a longing…

A Creator's Prayer

Great Creator and Supreme Artist

In the beginning,
Only *sabda*
The Sound.
Yet, a strange silence
Nishabdam.

Help me
To begin from the very beginning.
From this sacred space.
Every time I write,
Every moment of my life…
Now… Now… Now…
Help me to align
With your sacred energy,
GODhead
Good Orderly Direction
Even in chaos.
Direct me to
the magnetic centre -

still, silent space
where you reside,
reclining on *Ananta.*

Like the spider,
Centre me
In
(equanimity)
Shantam (stillness).

Let me weave your tapestry
And offer it to you -
A garland of wild flowers
From your *nandavanam,*
Sacred grove.

From one creator to another
It seems natural
To seek your help in this creative alliance.
I have faith you will…
As always.

Ekalavya

I can never be
Your Arjuna.
Kaladosha—the vagaries of time?
Maybe.
Karmic destiny?
I don't know.
I no longer want to know.
But this, I do know…
I accidentally
Gazed at you -
Your *pratibimbam,*
Your reflection
In the lake.
Lovingly… longingly… furtively…
Renuka, my friend,
Encouraged the gazing.
"You'll see yourself,"
She whispered.

Renuka, the wise elder,
Showed me how to mould clay.
"Your favourite," she again whispered.

And I…
I sculpted
Your earthen image.
Infused *prana,*
Grounded you
In the *garbha griha* –
The innermost sanctum of my temple.

You came alive
Crackled with vitality.
I saw you
You saw me
That *darshan*
That moment of seeing, knowing,
Is enough for me.
Arjuna's loss, my gain.
Gurudakshina?
I will give unasked.
Unlike Ekalavya.

Warp and Weft

Let me again fling
The warp and weft
Into the ocean.
Carelessly flung and spread
Against the oceanic expanse.
Like my sari *pallu*
Casually draped
Over my stooping shoulders,
Held in place
By your appraisals.

That hint of a smile;
That glimmer of recognition.

The thousand eyes of the peacock,
The warp and weft of my tapestry,
The wild flowers, my motifs
In my handwoven
Handblocked
Handdyed
Organic cotton sari.

Draupadi's Discovery

Wild, wayward, whimsical…
Like the wild flowers,
Her seeds of sorrow,
Pollinated by the birds and bees,
Drenched the earth
Like gentle rain -
Her silent sorrow.

The music of the rain,
This elemental dance
Of strange *saptaswara*
Unheard, unsung -
Saraswati strumming
On her tongue.
Like the wild flowers
She remained
Embedded underground.
Until, one day,
She bloomed.
Such strange splendour.
A wordless knowing

From within her
Emerged from
Silent spaces
Lingering inside her
Crevices. Cracks,
Fissures, fractures,
Fractals,
Cleaved her apart
Into millions of stars.
Sacred spaces within her
That called the wild flowers
From afar.

Not many know of her sorrow,
Her struggles,
Her strife,
Her camouflage,
Her ally, Nature's montage.

Wild flowers bloomed
From a grief within
That ripped her apart.

It takes deep sorrow
To rise again.

To savour the
Ecstasy of joyous wonder;
To embrace life
Daring to live again.

Deeply rooted in her knowing
She bloomed like wild flowers
Rising stronger like never before,
Soaring like the peregrine -
A sacred wanderer.

Draupadi's flowers,
The wild flowers.
Her *Saugandika;*
Her *Kurukshetra;* her *Dharma kshetra.*

Gajendra's Offering

She roamed, she wandered,
Soaring like Garuda
On the wings of her sorrow.

Her wingspan,
His infinite splendour
Her sanctuary.
Stronger, swifter than ever
She flowed.
Stronger than the rocks,
Deeper than the slopes,
Fluid as the Himalayan rivers in spate.

Seeta's sorrow -
Her mother's furrow…
She plumbed the depths
Where she met
Mahabali, the wise elder.

A sacred solitary reaper,
She harvested wild flowers
Wrapped in gossamer spider webs
Dyed in rainbow colours.
She showered
A floral frenzy -
Gajendra's piety
Cascading on His *Tirumeni*.
Her pain, her petals,
His *Kaustuba* -
Her crest jewel.

Stains

Your memory stains
Permanent markers
On my whiteboard.

Sacred Geometry

Bees droning
Mandalas of our making up
in sacred geometry.

Marinated

Marinated memories
Spread out in the sun
Shrivelled prunes.

Ambush

You lurk
In every unsuspecting
Pore of my being.
Crouching
Hidden,
Camouflaged,
Poised to pounce.

You've laid
Invisible landmines -
Detonate
Explode
Evade
My every attempt
To sidestep,
Dodge
This implosion,
Ambushed by predatory grief.

Oblivion

Poised on a leaf,
Crushed cotton scalloped wings
Blur of oblivion.

Suspension

Perpendicular
Suspended trapeze artiste
sun-kissed, sun-dried wings.

Yearning

Grief :
A yearning Saurus crane
Anticipating her lover.

Eclipse

Car crash;
Full moon in my purple night sky
Eclipsed forever.

Complications

Our complicated status:
Constants, straight lines
Black or white.
Her betrayal:

variables… curves…
a million shades of grey

Horizon
Old blue inland letter
tantalizing like the horizon;
you recede.

Melting moments
Angled light of the setting sun;
your head resting on my shoulder;
melting moments.

Wetness
Sanguine wetness…
the earth blotting
the ocean.

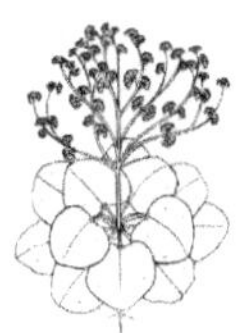

Afterword

Valiant, vulnerable and a radiant gift

> "Your absence has gone through me
>
> Like thread through a needle.
>
> Everything I do is stitched with its color."
>
> – W.S. Merwin

A present absence infuses each word of Nandini Murali's poignant collection of verses. Her earlier book, *Left Behind: Surviving Suicide Loss,* details her journey through the disorienting wilderness of suicide bereavement. It drives home, with candour and precision, the complex ramifications of suicide loss, and the damaging stigma, shame and silence that surround it.

Left Behind lights a way forward for survivors of suicide loss, their extended communities, and society at large. It is at once profoundly personal and deeply practical, and yet—the language of prose can only hold so much. The rest can only be approached through poetry and the silence from which all words spring. It makes perfect sense then, that Nandini chose to craft *Amidst the Wild Flowers* as a companion book to *Left Behind.*

These poems communicate to us from the sacred, searing, alchemical depths of human love, loss and longing. Through them, Nandini sings into the implacable void. She sings as a woman, wife, soulmate and seeker. And through this singing, she explores the landscape of her grief. She gives language to its haunting emotions, describes its intimate contours, and names its singular desolations and solaces.

Certain lines ambush the reader. Take, for example, one of the early poems in the collection:

The scent on your shirt

Lingers,

Reluctant to leave -

Unlike you

Who vanished

Like a leopard.

Here, in just a handful of words, Nandini juxtaposes domestic imagery with a stunningly abrupt jungle simile. The quiet finality of the leopard's vanishing registers like a gut punch. This verse, like many of the poems in this collection, reminds us that the wilds are not somewhere "out there." No. They lurk on our doorstep and reside in our very bones. Civilization may give us some illusion of control but ultimately we are part of an enigmatic universe where creation and dissolution are immutable laws of nature.

Author Rachel Naomi Remen writes that grieving is, "*...a sorting process. One by one you let go of the things that are gone and you mourn for them. One by one you take hold of the things that have become a part of who you are and build again.*" In the midst of unfathomable loss, Nandini's poems do exactly that. They are a valiant, vulnerable, and fiercely honest form of meaning-making. In them, Nandini aches for the disappeared love of her life, while simultaneously negotiating a radically transformed identity, and discovering her deepened capacities for wonder and reverence.

The vocabulary of Nandini's own spiritual path weaves through her poems, evoking the connection between the mortal, the mythic and the mystical. In distilled words, insights and images, she bears witness, not just to the physical sensations and energies of grief, but also to how it imprints the mind and psyche, and how it ignites the soul's journey. In this way, her book is an *Adipradakshina* unto itself—a "step-by-step pilgrimage," towards true spiritual union.

Nature in her many-splendoured manifestations becomes a fertile sanctuary of revelation for Nandini, and a recurring theme in these poems. The motif of wild flowers in her verses is moving and apt. Francis Weller writes, "Grief is suffused with life-force… It is not a state of deadness or emotional flatness. Grief is alive, wild, untamed and cannot be domesticated." This slender book of poems is infused with that kind of wild vitality.

Like Nandini's presence in our world, it too is a radiant gift.

– Pavithra Mehta

Belmont, California

Pavithra Mehta is a writer, documentary filmmaker and co-author of the highly acclaimed *Infinite Vision: How Aravind Became the World's Greatest Business Case for Compassion*

A gazelle on a mission

For anyone who has had the pleasure of reading Dr. Nandini Murali's self-searching memoir, *Left Behind: Surviving Suicide Loss,* her new book of poems *Amidst the Wild Flowers* arrives in the guise of a different delight. It is a veritable smorgasbord of emotions, truths, and glimpses into feelings and memories that cannot be erased by the passage of time.

I periodically revisit *Left Behind* for personal reasons. Each time I read a chapter that I have read before, a new nuance leaps out of the pages. Unlike so many authors of this age, Nandini Murali writes from her heart more than from her head. Her account of how she dealt with the loss of her beloved husband to death from suicide is sheer poetry written with a splash of blood.

The passion, the pain and the hope that pervades her writing could have only had its genesis in the cauldron of loss. I highly recommend *Left Behind* to anyone trying to get over loss of any kind, left feeling hopeless and that life will be barren forever. Nandini affirms that a new landscape awaits us.

To consolidate that belief, Nandini Murali has presented a close-up on the regenerative prowess and power of the mind with an anthology of her poems, *Amidst the Wild Flowers,* that explores love, loss and longing. This anthology of poems from Nandini vividly reaffirms the resilience hidden within all of us.

Nandini Murali pours her heart out with sixty-one poems, short and long, starting with cobwebs of the past that cannot be easily swept away and embers of memory that only remain as sacred ash. Nandini, once again, opens her life, her thoughts, her regrets and her resolve in every verse and every line. It is nothing short of amazing that she can put so much feeling into so few words.

The title reflects the regenerative challenges that can be overcome even in a land rendered barren by a feeling of sorrow that can never be measured in words—the loss of a spouse to death by suicide. These wild flowers that have blossomed in her garden of words and verses are filled with beauty but are also tinged with sadness, tears and fears.

But there is humour too—as seen in the *Vertigo of grief* written tongue-in-cheek, bound to bring a smile to the reader! In several of her poems, there are allusions to her faith that got her through her oceanic cataclysm. She walks a thin line from being very personal to being very non-personal. She does not shy away from sensitive and uncomfortable topics. In fact, she addresses them head-on, and with bold courage as seen in her poems, *Menage trois* and *Post coital slumber.*

The anthology of poems takes the reader on a whirlwind ride reserved for fantasy seekers. In one verse, we are left on the ground shedding a solitary tear and. in the next, we are flying on gossamer wings, leaping off the ground like a gazelle on a mission. The grandeur of her poetry and her command of the English language flow like a river—as seen in the poem, *Intransitive verb.*

While intrinsically each poem is in and of itself a gem in a treasure chest, some will be etched in memory. This, of course, will depend on the individual reader's intellectual terrain. To me what struck a chord most was her reference to the "phantom limb". The image of having lost the love of one's life and of groping to find the surgically amputated limb casts a spell on anyone who has lost a part of themselves but believes it to be present. As if that is not enough, Nandini Murali, for good measure, throws at us the image of the traumatized one, the one left behind, coiling and twisting and watching rehashed memories devoured and regurgitated by a python, no less. This is on par with anything Dante would have contrived.

I could go on and on, but constraints of time and space limit me. Suffice to say that with her body of work, Dr. Nandini Murali should be a well-deserved addition to the pantheon of respected writers and poets from India, or for that matter, from anywhere in the world.

**– Dr. C.R. Kannan is an author and
well-known US-based senior endocrinologist**